SO YOU WANT TO BE A CELEBRITY?

SO YOU WANT TO BE A CELEBRITY?

STEVE ALLEN

LEADING BRITAIN'S CONVERSATION
DAB DIGITAL RADIO | 97.3 FM

&

First published 2015 by
Elliott and Thompson Limited
27 John Street
London WC1N 2BX
www.eandtbooks.com

ISBN: 978-1-78396-107-8

9 8 7 6 5 4 3 2 1

A catalogue record for this book is available from the
British Library.

Managing Editor, LBC: James Rea
Deputy Managing Editor, LBC: Tom Cheal

Typesetting: Marie Doherty
Printed in the UK by TJ International Ltd

global

Contents

Introduction

First, a declaration: I am not a celebrity, I have never been a celebrity, I have no desire to become a celebrity. I have my own radio programme, I've been on the telly now and again, I've done a one-man show and other bits and pieces. What I am is a professional presenter. A celebrity is something quite different.

The most obvious example of modern celebrity is Jordan. She was once famous for doing something, but I can't imagine many people remember what it was (it was Page Three — classy). These days, her most recent desperate attempt to stay relevant, or at least noticed, was to scream about her current husband (Kieran, at the time of writing) having had affairs with two women. Poor Kieran can't help himself though, because he's a sex addict, so she'll forgive him. The women, on the other hand, she has slated as home-wrecking tramps. They slept with her husband while she was pregnant. How low can they go? Jordan doesn't seem to consider that they might have sex addiction problems of their own. Or that Kieran may just be a bit of a dog. Not that any of it matters — what's important to Jordan is that it's another bit of her life she can sell to the papers.

Celebrity, as a concept, is nothing new. In Roman times an emperor would have his head on coins, and that was a kind of fame, a type of celebrity, because it meant people knew who he was and what he looked like. Then, in time, the most successful gladiators got to have their faces on coins too and, looking back, we can see where celebrity began. Years later, Henry VIII would have audiences at Hampton Court who would pay money to stand behind a barrier and watch him eat. They couldn't address him, they couldn't interrupt him, they just paid their money and stood there, watching a man — their king — eat. These days, the modern equivalent is probably Prince Charles' banquets for the Prince's Trust benefactors. They pay a lot of money and they get to watch their prince — possibly their future king — eat. It's the same thing, except that he probably talks to them, and they get to eat too, which is a nice improvement.

It may go back further than the Romans — it's quite possible that there were caveman celebrities. Who's to say that whoever did the best bison cave-paintings wasn't a celebrated and feted person, sitting at the mouth of their cave, accepting freshly slaughtered woolly mammoth from the less talented. The point is, there has been a human desire for some kind of fame, of recognition, for as long as there has been humankind.

What we're talking about here is the most recent, modern, twenty-first century version.

1
What do I mean by celebrity?

By 'celebrity' I mean the current phenomenon of being famous for being famous. A person who started off as someone 'ordinary', someone any of us could know, someone who could live next door to you. Someone who doesn't necessarily have any skills or talents for the kind of things that would traditionally have led to fame. The person on the celebrity panel game who makes you think, 'Who the hell is that?' This is a modern celebrity. This is what, it seems, anyone can be. As long as they're prepared to put in the work.

This particular breed of celebrity probably started with Viv Nicholson in 1961. She famously won £152,319 on the football pools (a way of betting on the outcome of several football matches on one day) and when asked what she would do with it, declared loudly that she would 'Spend, spend, spend!' The papers loved her devil-may-care attitude, which went against the grain at a time when nobody had any money. The press followed her every move — the shopping trips, the holidays. The truth was, her husband had actually won the money and, until

3

his death four years later, he kept her under control. After he died, though, she was on her own and, within a short time, she had spent what today would be £2.87 million, and was declared bankrupt. But she'd had a taste, and over the next couple of decades she kept desperately trying to rekindle the fame she had relished. She recorded a single (called 'Spend, Spend, Spend'), sang 'Big Spender!' in strip clubs and wrote an autobiography. In the late nineties, a musical based on her life ran successfully in the West End, giving her notoriety — her celebrity — one more spin.

We also had The Krays, who, had they ever left prison, would certainly have had their own celebrity. As it was, they were the stuff of legend, with people saying how 'they'd never hurt their own', seemingly not caring that they'd hurt, and even killed, people who were somebody else's.

And then there were the Great Train Robbers, who were famous for stealing the equivalent of £46 million from a Royal Mail train, and bashing the driver over the head with a metal bar. It was 1963, and already celebrity was coming in the strangest of forms. There was a film about one of them, Buster Edwards. He was played by Phil Collins and it was quite a big deal of a film, but I still used to see him every day at Waterloo Station, selling flowers. I thought that must make him happy, but then I wondered if he missed his 'exciting' life of crime, and that's why he ended up hanging himself in a lock-up garage. This would be our first hint that a certain kind of celebrity may not always be that great.

In the 1980s, Cynthia Payne — Madame Cyn, as the press called her — was famous for running a brothel in suburban south London. She was very good on chat shows and her naughtiness titillated a nation raised on Carry On films. How much of what she said was true we never got to grips with, but nobody seemed to mind, and of course the story eventually culminated in a film about her, *Personal Services*, starring Julie Walters. It was a good film, and Cynthia seems to have been content with her allotted time in the spotlight. She faded politely from our consciousness without embarrassing herself.

And so to now, the twenty-first century, ushered in by the BBC's *Castaway 2000*, which was the first programme where they sent people away — in this case for a year, to a remote Scottish island. We have to assume these people didn't want to become celebrities, that their intention was to take part in a fascinating experiment, but, as we know, that's not how it ended. One person caught the public's imagination and lo, we had our first reality-TV star in Ben Fogle. His family weren't new to public attention as his mother had been famous; she'd starred with Tommy Steele in *Half a Sixpence* back in 1967. So maybe that helped, but whether it did or not, Ben Fogle was the first real breakthrough reality star, and the TV channels were quick to realise how compelling — and cheap — this kind of television could be.

We had the first *Big Brother* that year as well, which was also a kind of experiment — put a load of strangers in a house filled with hidden cameras, don't let them out, and see how they survive. The first one was brilliant, because nobody understood the game yet, and the behaviour of the contestants was genuine and fascinating. Once they came out, however, the attention they all got was unparalleled — our innocence was gone, and we were primed for an explosion: the advent of the new celebrity.

2
What celebrity used to mean

In the old days, celebrities were famous for doing something. Achieving something. For acting or singing, designing clothes, even writing in some cases. There were rock stars, pop stars, but the biggest stars, the ones who really were larger than life, were the movie stars. People like Rita Hayworth, Joan Crawford, Rock Hudson, Jimmy Stewart, Marilyn Monroe, Bob Hope, Deanna Durbin ... The list is endless. And we had British ones, too — Diana Dors, Julie Christie and Andrews, Alec Guinness, Richard Burton, John Gielgud, Laurence Olivier, Terry Thomas ... Cary Grant is technically one of ours too, as is Liz Taylor. Movies went around the world, so the stars who were in them became huge. And without the Internet to tear them down, we didn't know their secrets; they kept their mystery. They were untouchable and special and we adored them, just as their publicity demanded we should.

The pop singers of the day were big news, but not as big as the movies. Bill Haley and His Comets were the first American rock and roll stars to tour Britain, which they did in 1957, to almost hysterical crowds. Less than twenty years later they were back doing *The Wheeltappers and Shunters Social Club* — a naff British variety show in the mid-1970s — with hardly anybody caring. Even back then, celebrity could be a cruel mistress.

A British movie star who did very well in Hollywood was David Niven, notable for writing the bestselling celebrity autobiography *The Moon's a Balloon*. After its runaway success, the autobiography became another way for actors to tell their stories the way they wanted them told. How easy things were before the Internet. If not for the original gossip columnists, Hedda Hopper and Louella Parsons, who wrote what they wanted when they wanted and didn't care who they hurt, the old-time stars really would have been able to keep all their secrets. Until their children were old enough to tell their own versions, that is. This happened most famously with Joan Crawford's daughter, Christina, who wrote about what a terrible and abusive mother

Crawford had been in her bestselling memoir, *Mommie Dearest*, published in 1978. It shattered Crawford's reputation and caused a terrible rift in their family, with two sisters declaring it a fabrication, while their brother agreed that it was all true. Perhaps it's better these days, with the accusations coming from strangers sitting at computer keyboards.

What all these stars had was longevity. One good way of achieving this is dying young — not the best career choice, but it can work. Elvis Presley is the obvious one; had he not died young, would he be doing Vegas six nights a week? Probably. Look at Sinatra, a star who was still working until the day he dropped. You'd think, with the huge back catalogue of singers like these two, their forever stardom was always assured, and maybe that's true, but remember they didn't necessarily own the rights to their material, and that's where the cash is. When Elvis died, there was very little money in the pot. It had all been spent, and he owed a fortune, but he was loved, his fans were and still

13

are very loyal, so when Priscilla made the wise move to open Graceland as a tourist destination, the fortunes of the Presley estate were assured.

That kind of celebrity is about longevity. The Beatles are another example, where the only two still alive — Paul McCartney and Ringo Starr — are a bit embarrassing, whereas the two who have died, George Harrison and John Lennon, are seen as kind of heroic. Still, as someone who did write his own material, I don't imagine McCartney minds too much. And Harrison did well too; he wrote 'Here Comes The Sun' and, more famously, 'Something', which has been covered by over 150 artists, including Presley and Sinatra. I actually always wanted to visit George's house, Friar Park, because he had something amazing and unique there: his own underground waterways beneath the house, which I always imagined to be like the lakes in *Phantom of the Opera*, with little boats all lit up floating around. Imagine seeing that. Imagine having that in your house. That's proper stardom.

So that's what I think celebrity used to be. I'm not sure, because it's too early to tell, if we've got any around at the moment who could ever be as big. But I'll take a chance and suggest that the ones who retain the mystery, about whom we don't know that much, will be the ones we still hear about in decades to come. People like Adele, James McAvoy, Maggie Smith, Keira Knightley, Ian McKellen, George Clooney, Emma Thompson, Julia Roberts, Maggie Gyllenhaal — the ones who are great at what they do and don't call the press to let them know where they're having dinner that night. The ones who do their job and then go back home.

Strangely enough, I think if you asked the British public to name our biggest stars, they'd probably say Posh and Becks. They play a very clever game — we know loads about them, but they still have this mystery. We don't understand their relationship, but they seem committed to each other and their family. Once you know everything, people become a bit boring. There was a time when the Royal Family seemed mysterious; they had all this history that we learned about in school, which made them seem important and fascinating, and then they did a documentary and then, even worse, they did a ridiculous game show (*The Grand Knockout Tournament* — Google it), and it was all over. We knew too much.

In the old days of Hollywood, it was up to the studios what got out about their stars. They controlled information and nobody crossed them. Nowadays, with the Internet, even if something's not true, certain 'journalists' will write it anyway, and then whoever it's about has to prove that it's wrong. It's terribly unfair really, but it's the way it is.

So becoming a star, the old kind of celebrity, is not easy. You need skill and talent and integrity, and that's absolutely not what we're talking about here. If you want to be that kind of celebrity, you'll be studying acting or singing or writing or designing, you'll be working in that medium already. You'll be talented. And you won't need a book like this.

3

Routes to becoming a celebrity

The most obvious route to celebrity, the one that's currently the very best way, is the reality TV show. It's certainly the fastest. Most of the celebrities who spring to my mind in this category are off *Big Brother*, *TOWIE*, or *Made in Chelsea* – shows where they point out that these are real people, but the stories may have been enhanced for your entertainment. Slightly scripted reality TV, they call it, or at least some do. There are other reality shows, like *Come Dine with Me*, and *Four in a Bed* — a show that's about B&Bs, with a deliberately grubby-sounding title — that you can do, if all you want to do is be on telly for a week, but they're unlikely to make you into a celebrity, and going on them doesn't show real commitment to wanting to become one. It's a temporary thing, and it might mean you're recognised in your local high street for a few weeks, but it's rarely going to give you anything more permanent. If that's good enough for you, go ahead and enjoy. If you want more, if you want real modern celebrity, based on no skills at all, keep reading.

To get on a show like *TOWIE* or *Made in Chelsea*, you need to be part of the group the TV channel has decided to show, and that's not really very likely. It doesn't always work either — I can't name anybody from *Geordie Shore*, can you? — so as well as being lucky enough to be in the right gang, you also need to be lucky enough that the show you're in is one of the ones the media pick up on. And then you need to have an edge that makes you stick out from the other cast members so that you're the one who gets the media attention. One of the girls from *TOWIE* was in her underwear in the *Daily Star* recently — if you're going this route, try not to do that, or at least do it for the *Telegraph*. Think of your parents. But otherwise, it seems, anything goes. Although you'll be better off if you come up with something original, something unusual.

Having established the difficulty of and luck needed to get on a show like *TOWIE*, we need to look at other, more accessible options. *Big Brother* is one. From what we've seen in recent years, it seems anyone can get on that.

Though the gobbier or slightly weirder you are, the better. The days when Pete with Tourette's was a novelty are long gone. Now you need to be rude or dirty, have contentious opinions or no manners. Though you could try being the opposite — they like the odd posh-seeming person too, and they're unlikely to check if it's genuine.

The audition process for *Big Brother* is gruelling — interview after interview, all on camera, some with other potential housemates, some on your own. Each year thousands apply, and less than twenty will be on our screens all summer. But if you're determined, if you can portray a persona you think the producers will buy into and, more importantly, the viewing public will love or love to hate, then you have as much chance as anyone else. Hopefully a little more, if you read to the end of this book.

Then there are the talent shows. We've already established that you don't really have a talent, and luckily for today's shows, you don't need one. You have just as much chance of getting a shot at becoming a celebrity by being spectacularly bad. Producers on television talent shows know this, and just getting to the televised auditions stage means they're watching you and are ready with the pen, paper and binding contract. You don't need talent, as such, but you could be the next 'Where's my keys, where's my phone?' guy, and a chance of celebrity will be yours for the taking. Just in case you capture the public imagination, just in case the media pick up on your particular brand of awfulness, just in case you do something bizarre enough that they might want to put you out there for your novelty value, the contract is there and you will belong to them. For as long as they can earn money out of you. But that works for you, too. They won't bother if there's no mileage in you, so you need to use them as much as they will use you, because as fast as they can pick you up, they can drop you again.

There's also, of course, the old-fashioned, more traditional route of sleeping with a properly famous person and selling your story to the red tops. It's a bit tired and hackneyed, but it still works because sex still sells, especially if you've had it with someone everybody's heard of. Especially if they're married.

A successful actor or pop star will get you money and a story in a tabloid, but the real score is the famous footballer. That's where the big story is. It's also a lot easier — actors and pop stars are more careful these days, but footballers are still ordinary guys who get paid an extraordinary amount of money for kicking a bit of leather around. They can go to the clubs, spend a fortune on Cristal for all the pretty girls and after a few glasses of that, they're fair game. With the best will in the world, these guys earn crazy money. Look at Wayne Rooney — he's said to be on £300,000 a week. That's over a million a month. Of course these are the guys the public love to read about screwing up. And then, the moment you become famous for selling your story, you pose in your underwear and you're on your way. It doesn't really matter what you look like, as long as you don't mind getting your kit off in the papers, but if you are lucky enough to look good in a thong, this could be where you get lucky — you could get picked up by Victoria's Secret or Michelle Mone might ask you to model her bikini line, and you're off.

You could just go to the right nightclub and hope to get lucky if you're choosing this route, but sometimes a bit of diligence can pay off. I knew a girl once who would go to nightclubs on the nights she knew there were lots of celebrities in and she'd make sure to meet as many of them as possible, write all their details down, then go home and research them. She'd find out which ones had already had stories sold on them, which ones were the richest, which ones were and weren't worth hanging around. Then, the next time she went, she could dismiss the ones that weren't successful or rich enough, and deliberately target the ones who would get her the best deal if she could snare them. She would know who and what they liked, and would make herself appear to be the kind of person who they would be attracted to, without them having any idea of who she really was. Until they opened the papers the day after they'd slept with her. It is bizarre, but it can work.

Finally, there is what I'm calling the 'oddities' category. And the two examples I immediately think of both have similar names, though it isn't actually necessary to be called Josie or Jodie.

Jodie Marsh was one of the earliest famous-for-being famous nightclub girls. At a time when women usually went out fully dressed, she would get herself photographed in the doorways of nightclubs wearing very little. The big breakthrough came for her when she wore a belt diagonally across her otherwise naked torso, covering her nipples, and that was about it. She was fake-tanned and high-heeled and her unique selling point was, bizarrely, that her (large) boobs were real. Never mind that her tan wasn't real, and her nose wasn't real — her bust was, and that was worth shouting about. It was an obvious jibe at Jordan, who by then had famously had at least one set of improbably huge implants.

Jodie was photographed enough at one nightclub that other clubs started to offer her money to come and be photographed with hardly any clothes on at theirs, too. And so her irritating 'career' began. Like all the most successful celebrities, she kept coming up with things for the papers to talk about; she posed topless in lads' mags, did Page Three, got her own reality show, went on other 'celebrity' reality shows and, most recently, has taken up bodybuilding and being tattooed, giving her a whole new physical look to exploit. Jodie is quite a success at doing what she has chosen to do.

And then we have the most recent famous-for-being famous person. At least, at the time of writing. If you read as much gossip press as I do — and I'm as fascinated and disgusted as the next person — you'll know all about Josie Cunningham. But in case you only have a vague knowledge of her, and as a lesson in how to get famous for absolutely nothing but audacity, here's the route she's taking. She first came to public attention in 2009 for getting a boob job on the NHS. Quite how she pulled that off is anybody's guess, but after that she went quiet until she came hurtling into our consciousness again when she told the press she was prepared to have an abortion in order to get on *Big Brother*. Fearing adverse publicity, the programme put out a statement that they weren't planning on having her on, whether she had an abortion or not.

With that avenue closed, she then claimed she was not going to give up smoking or drinking as she'd discovered the baby was going to be a boy. She was very angry because a psychic had apparently told her it would be a girl and now it was too late to have an abortion (although in the end it did turn out to be a girl). She also had a tooth straightened on the NHS (because she's pregnant) and for a while claimed the state was paying for her to travel everywhere by taxi due to the panic attacks she gets on public transport because she's so hated. More hated than Jordan, is her claim. Who she also intends to be 'bigger than'. I think she means in terms of public awareness, but who knows. She then said they wanted her to be on *Celebrity Big Brother* but weren't offering her enough money.

If this is true, it is the worst side of celebrity culture; when reality shows have celebrity editions featuring people who are famous for being on reality shows, one has to wonder where it will all end. It has happened before, of course, but more of that later. We've also been told that Josie Cunningham has been offered a book deal, because she wants to tell us 'the truth'. I don't want to know the truth! If this is true, it has to make her the most successful modern celebrity in that she has actually done nothing but be hideous in order to achieve her celebrity dream. And it's worked. So that's another way to go. Although you'll have to come up with something even more bizarre, and you'll also have to not mind being universally despised. I doubt there's a single person who knows about her who doesn't detest Josie Cunningham.

4

After you get your break

So, you're going to be on telly. On *The X Factor* maybe, or on *Britain's Got Talent*, or your story about sleeping with a footballer is in the press. Maybe you've got to know someone from *TOWIE* or *Made in Chelsea* and you're going to be in an episode. Hell, you may even have just come up with a story the press love, like Samantha Brick did. Whatever it is, you're going to get noticed, and you need to strike while the iron's hot. You need to make sure you do something that makes you stand out, that gives you an edge.

Let's start with Samantha Brick, because she managed to get her fame by not having done any of the things we've talked about. In 2012 she wrote a piece that the *Daily Mail* published, saying that she was so beautiful that other women despised her, and airline pilots gave her free champagne just for being on their plane. Now, my mother would always say, 'You have to be nice to people. Be nice.' And I do try, but, of course, she really wasn't most people's idea of beautiful, so the nation reacted in horror and disgust, and we all thought, 'But you're *not* beautiful. Surely nobody's told you that you are?' But because of that she was on all the talk shows, brazening it out and making her money while she could. She kept it going for a good while too, with lots of columnists trying to explain why it had happened, and keeping the story alive. Then she got *Celebrity Big Brother* — on the strength of saying she was so beautiful that her life was difficult, which clearly can't have been true.

It did quieten down in the end, but by then we all knew who she was, and most of us thought she was dreadful, although not because we found her too beautiful. She went on to write a piece about how 'people are very jealous of my husband', but by then we'd heard it all and the Brick phenomenon was over. That's how it can work. Presumably she's happy, living with her lucky husband and counting the extra cash her one outrageous claim has made her.

Most people don't get their ridiculous ideas reported in the *Daily Mail*, so that's not very likely to be a route you can take. More likely, you're on the telly and you need to get yourself noticed. You can do it in that 'Oh God, what an idiot' kind of way, like the Chawner family did. You probably remember the Chawners. Daughter Emma went on *The X Factor* to sing, back in 2007, when the auditions were still in front of the judges in a small room. She didn't sing very well, and it looked like she would just be another reject as the news was broken to her and she walked out, broken. But then her parents came in. And her sister. And they shouted at the judges, Simon in particular, that their daughter was indeed a brilliant singer and what did they know, etc. Cowell famously told the parents it was their fault their daughter thought she could sing, and labelled them a disgrace for telling her she had a talent she clearly didn't. The next year Emma was back, failed again, and then in 2009 she came on with her sister, and they still didn't get through. Because they still couldn't sing.

What I haven't mentioned yet is that the Chawner family was large. Every member was morbidly obese, and the papers were happy to

SO YOU WANT TO BE A CELEBRITY?

pretend to be as horrified by that as the audience were. Really, of course, we thought it was funny. We were laughing at this poor family making a show of themselves, and congratulating ourselves at not being so fat or so deluded.

The Chawners didn't mind that, though. They knew what they looked like, and they were happy to pose, smiling, for the *Daily Mail*, under headlines calling them 'The Real Telly Tubbies'. They seemed delighted to reveal their combined weight of 83 stone and declare themselves too fat to work. And then, in 2012, they got their own reality show, in which they dieted, tried to get jobs, and appeared to want to become useful members of society. Maybe people bought that, but whether they did or not, when it was over it seemed their notoriety had reached its natural end.

Until, early in 2014 they turned up on a show called *The Nightmare Neighbour Next Door*, apparently having had more than 600 complaints made about their unneighbourly behaviour. It seems this family will stop at nothing to get themselves on the television, and that's one way of becoming a celebrity. As with Josie Cunningham, though, the Chawners did it by being universally hated. That might not be the path you want to take, but it is there if you want it. If nothing else works, and you really want to be a celebrity at any cost.

At the other end of the scale, there's the Posh and Becks phenomenon that I've already mentioned. But I would like to give a nod to Posh and what a fantastic job she has done, with regard to creating the enormous worldwide celebrity of the Beckham brand. When the Spice Girls were big — and they were huge — Victoria was the least impressive of all of them, the one deemed 'unlikely to succeed'. And arguably she wasn't the biggest star of the five. But then David Beckham spotted her and marrying him changed everything.

This is when her talents became apparent — a canny businesswoman, a brilliant publicist and, as it turns out, a talented designer. But with the Beckhams you get family as brand, which was a new and clever spin on celebrity. She knows how to market them, how to keep David mysterious by not letting him speak about anything other than football. Apart from that, it's his look, his body, that does the talking, and it does it a lot better than his mouth.

Even now, she's making sure the world knows her kids aren't going to be spoiled and have an easy life: Brooklyn, the eldest Beckham son, is reportedly working for minimum wage in a coffee shop, so that he understands the value of money. Of course, earlier in 2014 he was modelling for *Man About Town* magazine, so he'll be experiencing both ends of the pay scale. What matters though, is that he's getting good press and keeping the brand Beckham name alive going into the next generation. She may have been the weakest link in the Spice Girls, but she's turned out to be the biggest star.

Unless you're already in a successful girl band, however, you're unlikely to be able to emulate Posh's success, and I'm guessing you don't really want to follow in the Chawners' footsteps either, so let's take a look at the middle ground with a few examples.

Firstly, and quite interestingly, there's the tale of Abi Titmuss. Just getting in before the advent of Google in our everyday lives, Abi Titmuss was originally noticed as the girlfriend of John Leslie, the ex-*Blue Peter* presenter. When he was accused of rape in 2003, she stood quietly by his side, accompanying him to court every day, saying little but appearing in every photograph of the beleaguered ex-presenter. When he was found innocent, his career in shreds, she declared her loyalty once more and was suddenly working as a roving reporter for Channel 4's *Richard and Judy* show.

Less than a year later, a fairly filthy sex tape came to light and she was sacked from that job, but went on to do glamour modelling, declaring herself to be 'really dirty and bad', and landing a job hosting on a porn channel. After a couple of years of that, she disappeared, returning a few years later as an actress. This is a woman who was trained as a nurse by the NHS, back in the days when we paid for their training. She cleverly linked up with a famous person and could never have dreamed how well that would work out for her. When she saw those opportunities, she jumped at them, and now, shockingly, has a career as an actress.

I once interviewed a very good actress, someone you'd recognise and respect, and she'd just done a play with Abi Titmuss. When it was over, the actress, who has worked in that field for years, had nothing else coming up, no work at all. Not terribly surprising these days; it's as tough out there for actors as for anyone else. The surprising thing was that Abi Titmuss had four offers before the play had ended. And one of them was to do Lady Macbeth.

Theatre doesn't really keep you in the public eye though, and Abi Titmuss knows that — she's done her share of 'celebrity' reality shows, including *Celebrity Come Dine With Me*, where we saw her flat. She obviously realised at least one of her fellow celebs didn't know who she was, so there were shots of her modelling all over the place. All this for playing the dutiful girlfriend who stood by her man, even when he was accused of the most heinous of crimes. The fact that he was found innocent helped, of course. But whatever the outcome, she'd still have played her part, still have been in the papers every day, and that was enough for a clever young woman to climb the ladder of fame.

As stories of how to achieve celebrity go, Abi Titmuss' is an impressive one. The fact that she realised the glamour/dirty girl stuff wasn't going to last and did a quick acting course speaks of a woman with ruthless ambition and no qualms about making it happen. This is a bit of a slow-and-steady road to celebrity, but it worked for her. Maybe it can work for you, if you find the right guy. Perhaps leave out the porny bit in the middle, though.

As an aside, from the point of view of an observer, I can't help but feel bad about some of these D-list celebrities having jobs fall into their laps. When being famous for getting your kit off gets you a well-paid role in panto, I have

39

to wonder how all these people struggling to pay their way through RADA and other acting schools must feel. But the celebs do get these roles, and they also get book deals, which has to be just as galling for experienced writers looking to get published. It's just the way it is.

But back to reality TV, and how you can work your way towards panto.

When *The Apprentice* first aired, it appeared to be a serious business programme, with just enough of a reality show element to make it interesting. Fascinating, in fact, given the high viewing figures it started to gather. And for the first two series it was just that: the winners gained their promised jobs in Alan Sugar's empire and the rest of us moved on when each series ended. Then came series three, and with it Katie Hopkins. Katie played the game on *The Apprentice* like it had never been played before, making nasty, cutting comments about her competitors to camera with barely disguised glee. The nation started to dislike her, in that way that we love to dislike people. It's not really something you can manufacture, that kind of hatefulness — sometimes we just hate people, but sometimes we *love* to hate them, and this is its own kind of TV gold.

Towards the end of the series, when Sir Alan offered her a place in the final, Hopkins shockingly rejected it, claiming she had childcare issues. She then spent as much time as she could telling anyone who would listen that she would surely have won, if she'd taken up the offer and been in the final.

She irritated people so much that properly successful people started to declare their hatred of her, including film-maker Richard Curtis, who joked about killing her. On Hopkins' episode of *The Apprentice*'s sister programme, *You're Fired*, Michelle Mone, owner of lingerie brand Ultimo, told her, 'You've given businesswomen a bad name.' Ironic really, as Hopkins' only business to date has run at a net loss since 2009, has negative net worth and, at the time of writing, has declared zero turnover for the past two years. But the media is never known to let the facts get in the way of a good story, and Hopkins is still introduced on the shows she appears on as a businesswoman. And that's her real career — being gobby and offensive, contentious for its own sake, some might say, on talk shows.

Not quite as clever as she thinks she is, Katie famously declared that she judges her children's classmates according to their first names. She sneered that she would never let her children play with anyone called Tyler or Chardonnay, and then got so into her stride that she clearly wasn't concentrating when she said how ridiculous she thought it was to name a child after a geographical location. Immediately seeing her screw-up, the presenters pointed out that she has a daughter named India, and she became furious: how dare they bring her child into this, how very disgusting of them. Never mind that she'd spent the last few minutes slagging off children quite possibly in her daughters' classes at school.

After a fight with Peaches Geldof about parenting went spectacularly badly for her, with

Peaches clearly winning that particular debate, Katie Hopkins disappeared from our screens. Not one to be taken down that easily, she took to Twitter to spew her outrageous hate-filled tweets. Mostly you think, 'That's just a stupid thing to say' and move on, but there are always people ready to try to take her down, retweeting her to everyone, and thus she still gets attention. The papers seem to publish a selection of her hateful tweets every few weeks, so she remains in the public eye. Still, she is a celebrity. So that could be a way to go, if you feel you can handle it. And have the capacity to be that unpleasant, of course.

Of course, you don't have to be particularly clever or educated to get your break. The biggest breakthrough star of *TOWIE* is probably the fortunately named Joey Essex (it really is his real name), who is mostly renowned for not being very bright. It comes to something when that's your edge, but who am I to judge what works? Somebody's advising Joey very well, because he wasn't an original cast member, appearing as a supporting player in series two, and finally being promoted to a main cast member in series three. Two years later, he left the show and was next seen diving into a pool on *Splash!*, the Tom Daley series in which celebrities learned to dive and then competed with each other. He didn't get very far in that, but he really caught the public imagination when he appeared on *I'm A Celebrity Get Me Out of Here*, when a whole new audience sat, awestruck, at his guileless lack of knowledge. Most notably when he confessed that he didn't know how to tell the time, and had to be taught how to by a glamour model.

His sister is also a *TOWIE* cast member but she doesn't have the magic her little brother does. As well as being spectacularly uneducated, Joey seems to have a heart of gold; he appears genuinely decent and caring and somehow that combination is working wonders for him. He's appeared on *Celebrity Juice* five times in two years, been on all manner of other celebrity shows and after a one-off documentary in which he went to South Africa and gazed, open-mouthed, at everything he saw there, someone at ITV2 was so charmed they ordered a full series. So Joey Essex became kind of a travel journalist — surely even his agent couldn't have seen that coming.

Like many of his fellow cast members, Joey has launched his own beauty products — in his case, a haircare line called D'Reem Hair — and has also opened a men's fashion boutique in Brentwood called Fusey. When he opened it, the other shopkeepers on the street complained bitterly that they couldn't get to their shops because of all the tourists who were coming down to see Joey Essex in a shop the size of a small bedroom. It sells men's clothes, but poor, dumb Joey doesn't know how to operate a till, nor does he have any idea what change to give a customer from a twenty-pound note when he has bought an item for a fiver. Seriously, a woman asked him and he just stood there, looking blank.

Joey Essex has probably never had a job, and I can't help thinking, 'You're going to go broke very quickly', and he would if he didn't have all this publicity. Which, eventually, he won't. In Joey's case, though, it won't matter, at least not for now, because he's still got his travel journalism gig. I'm not sure that if you were stupid enough to do what Joey Essex has done, you would know you were stupid enough to do what Joey Essex has done. I really think Joey's meteoric rise to D-list status may be a one-off. But, you know, it's there, and it's worked. And if, as some people have suggested, he's just pretending, he could genuinely have a career as a top-class actor.

So we've looked at a few options — being very clever, being very filthy, marrying well, and being so thick the world is in awe. What we haven't looked at is being nice. But the bad news is that this just doesn't work. To be successful, you need to have a bit of an edge, to have something else going on — whether you're a bit feisty, get a bit racy after a few drinks, or, god forbid, behave in a way that's wholly inappropriate. So, while being nice might serve you well in the world and might get you genuine friends and people who love you, might ensure that your passage through life is generally happy and hassle-free, it's unlikely to make you into a successful reality star.

Who wants to watch nice people? Snow White is nice. Lovely though she is, she wouldn't cut it as a modern celebrity.

5

I've done the first bit, what do I do next?

OK, so you've got on the show, you've sold the story, you don't want it to stop there and you need to find ways to maximise your impact. Sometimes, you need do nothing and it just happens for you. That's rare, and it's not something you should rely on if you're serious about wanting to be a celebrity, but someone who really didn't expect what happened to her was Jade Goody.

Goody went into the *Big Brother* house at a time when the nation was still watching the show — series three, probably the last one that 'everybody' saw — at just twenty years old. And she was awful. Dreadful. Not very bright, and quick to have a strop, or end up in tears. She famously thought East Anglia was called East Angular and wasn't a part of the UK. She believed Margaret Thatcher was a well-known prostitute and Rio de Janeiro was a person. The *BB* audience were as one: we hated her. We loved hating her (as discussed, that's the kind of hate you want if you're going to be a celebrity), and how much we despised her, how completely stupid she seemed, was the subject of daily discussions in offices across the land.

Back story is always useful if you want to get noticed, and Jade's was summarily dug up, revealing a father she barely knew, who was in prison, and a disabled lesbian mother who had brought her up alone. This was all reported with a very definite judgemental slant and we went along with it, until the *Sun* went too far. 'Vote out the pig' was their headline, focusing on Jade's looks and making references to 'trotters' and 'roasting' her. This was too much. You don't attack a twenty-year-old kid for her looks. The tide turned and everything we'd found horrific about her was suddenly charming and refreshing and sweet. When she came out of the *BB* house (coming fourth), it was to a wave of love and fondness and she was on chat shows and reality shows, giving interviews to the magazines and papers, her celebrity status assured.

At this point, she was cleverly advised and it seems she listened; we didn't see much of her on screen, but we read about her — about her relationship with ex-Leyton Orient footballer Jeff Brazier, their two children, their break-up, her new relationship … how she ran the marathon and collapsed, how she wrote her autobiography (which people must have read, or at least bought), released a perfume … and then she made a mistake. She went into the *Celebrity Big Brother* house.

Apart from this being like celebrity culture eating itself, it was never going to go well for Jade. We were reminded of her ignorance, her rudeness, her cocky mouthiness that seemed constantly angry, her penchant for slagging people off. This culminated in her calling Bollywood actress Shilpa Shetty ('beautiful Bollywood actress' as the papers would call her) Shilpa Poppadom. Trying to dig herself out of the mess, Jade just made things worse — on her own, with nobody to advise her and the country watching, Jade didn't have a prayer. She confirmed herself as a racist with every word that spewed from her angry mouth, and once again the press — and us — turned against her.

This time even the politicians joined in, and there were calls for the head of Channel 4 to resign. This was D-list celebrity at its most insane. Everything she'd worked for was under threat, and she came out this time to find herself an object of disgust. There wasn't even a crowd to greet her, as Channel 4 banned them for fear of an angry mob. Her stock was at an all-time low and it looked like her reign as super-celebrity was over. In an effort to mitigate all this, someone came up with the bizarre plan of putting her in the Indian *Big Brother* house, where she would be able to prove she wasn't a racist. Or something. Nobody really cared, but then there was another twist, when Jade was called into the diary room to be told that she had cervical cancer, and again a nation changed its mind about her.

It quickly became clear she wasn't going to beat the cancer, and her two little boys were set to be motherless. Determined to leave them as much money as she could, she set about selling what she had left of her life, ending by marrying her jailbird boyfriend in a lucrative deal with a magazine that gave them exclusive access to her wedding photos.

She died a month later, at just twenty-seven, having lived a celebrity life that couldn't have been much fun at times, but leaving a legacy that spoke well of her as thousands of young women, who may not otherwise have considered it, started getting tested for cervical cancer.

A final twist in Jade Goody's story emerged in 2013, when it was discovered that the one million pounds she had left for her boys' education was all going to be taken in lieu of the tax she hadn't paid. A cautionary tale of celebrity if ever there was one, Jade's story is worth thinking about before you decide if you really want to be a celebrity yourself. Fortunately, she was probably a one-off.

So this isn't likely to happen to you, and you probably wouldn't want it to, given how it ended. In which case, what do you do now you've secured your opportunity, your flash in the pan? How do you make it into something lasting?

Well, the answer is that you're not going to do it on your own, and the first thing you need is an agent. One of the most successful is Jonathan Shalit OBE (the OBE's a clue — he's so good at this, the Queen decided to honour him), so obviously that's who I had a chat with. Only the best for this book.

The first thing you should do is write to every agent you like the sound of when you know you're going to be in the public eye. Tell them what show you're on, what paper you're in, when it's going to happen, what you're good at, what you're prepared to do, and hope that one of them bothers to watch or read what you're selling.

Jonathan Shalit says that when he started in the business, he used to get letters from people telling him they were brilliant at what they do, accompanied by an example — a tape of their music, a show reel of their performing or presenting. They'd promote their talent, tell him what they were working on, pledge that they wanted to be the best in the world at their skill, and ask for his help to do that.

Nowadays, he gets letters and emails saying 'I want to be famous'. They add that they're prepared to work hard and do everything he asks, but they don't offer a talent or skill, just their desire to be famous. Their fantasy of being a celebrity. Shalit blames the gossip magazines for this phenomenon, this belief that anybody can be famous. He thinks they sell a make-believe lifestyle: 'They don't go to the toilet, they always look wonderful when they go to bed, they look wonderful when they get up … [people think] the fantasy life is real and they will dream of that, not realising it's virtually impossible to achieve.'

He says what he looks for is longevity — he accepts that there are people who are famous for being famous, but says that if someone has been in the public eye for more than five years, in the current marketplace, then that is somebody who should be respected. He admits that the word 'celebrity', in our terms, can be applied to some of his clients, but asserts that they are 'people with talent that I can look people in the eye and say I'm proud to represent'. He goes on to say that he knows I may disagree with him on that and boasts that two of his clients who work very hard are Myleene Klass, who we know is an extremely gifted musician, and Kelly Brook, a successful model and actress. He says again that they work very hard, unlike a lot of these kids who turn up in reality shows, become famous for a short while and then the moment passes.

These are the people we want to know about, though. The ones who get there with no history and no discernible talent. That's the route we're interested in, so I ask him how much people like that can earn, and it turns out to be rather a lot. Mostly for appearing in nightclubs. At the height of a TV show's popularity, he says, these people can earn £5,000 to stand around in a night-club, smile and be photographed with punters. £5,000. For doing virtually nothing except getting dressed and getting in a taxi. This is the kind of celebrity we're looking for. If you can get booked for two nightclubs on a Friday and two nightclubs on a Saturday, you'd earn £20,000 in one weekend. You do that for forty weekends in a year — because you can't do them all; you have to go to Marbella — that's £800,000. Just for going to nightclubs. And you'll probably get a few pics in the gossip mags and rags as well, which will keep you alive in the public consciousness. This can't go on forever though, surely? Shalit says no, he reckons that after the show you're on ends, or your stories are all sold, you've got about eighteen months of fame and then it's over. Unless you can find a way of extending it.

I ask if he sees this fascination with celebrity fading any time soon. He thinks not, and mentions a politician who has chucked it all in to become a celebrity, and wonders out loud whether someone like Jeremy Clarkson is a celebrity or a television presenter. There are other adjectives that may apply to Clarkson, but we ignore them. Shalit's point is that there's a constantly growing desire to fill pages and more and more people are needed to fill those pages on a continual basis. He adds that the mostly young readers have a limited attention span and can be very fickle; you may be loved for a while, but you could just as easily be out the window and replaced with the next new celebrity in a couple of days.

So now we know — make hay while the sun shines. While your show is on, or your story is current, grab every opportunity you can, be it nightclub appearances, the red carpet at premieres or talking to the Loose Women. As soon as you're not current, unless you're very lucky, you've got eighteen months of celebrity left.

6

What if it doesn't last?

8

What if it doesn't last?

What if it doesn't last? A good question, because almost inevitably it won't. We've discussed why, but what about trying to make it last? Trying to get to that elusive five years that Shalit mentioned. Well, there are options, though they may not be open to you. It all depends on how you've been portrayed. Oh, and that's not exactly up to you either — television shows will edit things to look the way they want them to, the press will cut and paste and rejig what you've said to make it suit the headline they fancy writing, and avoiding looking like an idiot is no easy task. But we're going to accept that you've tried your best, you've had a bit of fame, and your star is fading. What's next?

Well, firstly, you'll have put aside at least a third of your earnings for tax, won't you, because otherwise you'll end up in the press for that. And broke. Possibly bankrupt. There are people who make this their constant story, but they've usually had a bit of a career at the beginning — a few hits, say, like the boys from Blue and Kerry Katona, or a bit of presenting and acting like

Wendy Turner and her husband Gary Webster, who went bankrupt and then made money by writing a book about going bankrupt. Very brazen. And now it's been done, so that's not open to you. Definitely best, in your case, to put the money aside and be able to retreat back into uncelebrity with a shred of dignity. Part of that dignity will be doing the actual fading back into being unknown. That's a good thing to do — you've had the merry-go-round ride and now it's over. Hopefully you didn't just want to be famous and you'll have some job experience, a skill perhaps, maybe even a degree in something useful. At least a few A levels. If you saved your money, you could even learn a new skill — there's always a need for plumbers, for instance.

You might be thinking about the opening a shop option, *à la* the *TOWIE* gang. Well, don't. Those shops won't last long once their owners are no longer on the television, and there is evidence they are already failing in a couple of cases. At the height of his fame in 1994, Prince opened a shop in Camden selling memorabilia, which only lasted two years. Even The Beatles opened a shop, hoping to cash in on the total devotion of their fans. Their Apple Boutique opened in December 1967 in Marylebone, with the appealing concept of being 'a beautiful place where beautiful people can buy beautiful things'. It closed the following July. The Beatles. The first huge British pop phenomenon. And they couldn't make it work, so what hope do you have, with the little bit of celebrity you will achieve? You may have worked in a shop at one point, you may come from a family of retail geniuses, but if you're going to open a shop based only on the fact that you're a twenty-first-century celebrity, you are probably going to fail. Plumbing is still the more realistic choice.

There are those for whom fame is addictive. Who can't give it up, and will do, say or sell anything to keep it going. These are the people who feed the reality-TV monster at its most relentless. When Jordan met Peter Andre in the jungle on *I'm A Celebrity* ..., both of their stars were on the wane. Nobody's quite sure what Jordan was ever actually famous for, and Peter Andre had basically been amusingly well-muscled when he sang his song, 'Mysterious Girl', standing in a lake under a waterfall. Now Andre was working in his brother's gym and Jordan was struggling to keep her body in the press.

Who am I to question whether they genuinely fell in love or not, but certainly their getting together so publicly, with the world watching their romance blossom, gave both of their 'careers' the boosts they so desperately needed. And having started the whole thing in the public eye, that's where they made sure they stayed, with cameras following their every move, the births of their children, their outlandish wedding, their horrible duet of the Disney song 'A Whole New World', and the gradual and inevitable deterioration of the coupling.

After that, they both struggled to keep the public interest going, attacking each other ever more outrageously in an effort to keep themselves current. Andre was more careful about what he said, acted hurt in the face of Jordan's next marriage, and found public sympathy was on his side. He did more reality television, covering his brother's battle with cancer, the gym he'd worked in, holidays with his kids. To this day, he's still very present in the gossip mags, regularly on the cover of *OK!*, and is now fronting ITV's popular daytime show *Sixty Minute Makeover* or, as it's now called, *Peter Andre's Sixty Minute Makeover*.

Jordan, on the other hand, is behaving entirely more desperately. Suddenly insisting on now being called by her given name, Katie Price, she must have thought she could erase the perception of her being about boobs and babies, but it was not to be. She's still happy to sell the world her every move, even if a lot of people seem to have stopped buying. After having told anyone who'd give her five pence about her latest partner — and babydaddy — sleeping with her best friend, she then seemed to be floundering. We know everything about her, we've heard her every thought, and we're all Katie Priced out. People just don't seem to care as much any more. She went on to do a radio show where she tries to say outrageous things that will catch the public's imagination and make them give a monkey's about her again. She's going to have to do a bit better than declaring she never wears knickers. We'd probably have been more surprised if she'd said she sometimes does wear them.

Some celebrities whose time should really have been up, but who can't bear to let go, have come up with a new pathway to keeping their star shining — they are The Dieters. Top of the list on this one are Kerry Katona, who once had a career singing in Atomic Kitten and being married to a boy-bander from Westlife, Claire Richards, who used to be in nineties band Steps, and Chantelle Houghton, who ... Well, she was a pretend celebrity in *Celebrity Big Brother*, thus exposing the commitment to celebrity of the others, who were too embarrassed to admit they didn't know who she was. She then married fellow house-mate Preston, wrote an autobiography, divorced Preston and can now only dream of having the profile of Kerry Katona. But she's doing OK with the dieting thing too.

In all these cases, having babies has helped, and bought them a bit longer on the celebrity ride. Like Katona, Claire had a reality show for a brief while, though hers was only about dieting — how hard she found it, how hard her partner found it, how hard it was feeding her little boy when she was dieting. It exhausted the possibilities of making a reality show about a dieting celebrity and now these shrinking, ballooning, then shrinking again ladies make their money from the press. Katona is probably the biggest earner, reportedly getting paid a hefty sum by the *Sun* for her summer Sun diet. Don't be surprised if she porks up again in time for a Christmas diet. If Claire or Chantelle don't beat her to it.

In conclusion, if it looks like it isn't going to last, you do have options. It's up to you if you want to be the kind of person to take them.

7
The fascination with celebrity

Ah, if I could explain our fascination with celebrity, I'd earn a fortune, so what you're getting is my observations — some from where I sit as a presenter and interviewer, and some from reading the same stuff we all do, that we all can't help picking up, buying and devouring, whether with a sneer or a hunger for information.

We may be scathing about what we read, most particularly regarding the kind of celebrities we're talking about, but still we do it. Still we read, we buy into, we keep the whole culture of celebrity alive. And we do it willingly; nobody is making us. If we were to all stop buying *heat*, *Now*, *OK!*, *Closer* and *Hello*, then the industry would not be able to survive. If we stopped watching reality shows, the TV companies would eventually stop making them. Goodness knows, we have plenty of options when it comes to channels — some of them don't have reality shows on twenty-three hours a day, though admittedly many of them do. But we don't do these things, do we? We keep buying and we keep watching and the cult of the modern celebrity, of being famous for being famous, continues to grow. And that's why you have the opportunity to join it.

Be aware, however, that that's all it is. Celebrity. Even when it comes to TV talent shows, you're not getting credibility or fame. If you want to write your own music, to be a 'proper' musician, you wouldn't go near them. Because as a contestant on those shows you will do covers, you will do Abba night, and you may get a couple of hit songs, even an album out of it, but history shows that you will disappear and you are very unlikely to become a respected musician.

Sharon Osbourne points out, 'People forget who was on last year. It's all about the year that they're watching. There have been some superstars — but the majority are forgotten.' She adds that it is, as we know, 'fleeting, fleeting, fleeting'. And this is the key with all the competitive reality shows — as an audience we care, we really care, while it's on. We are interested in most of the players, we have our favourites, and those we enjoy despising; we will read about them, listen to TV reports on them, watch every episode, but the day a series finishes, our interest ends with it. We don't care about them any more. That passion we felt just twenty-four or forty-eight hours ago has vanished, and we are wondering — if we think about it at all — who will be on next year's show. That's what you need to overcome, to break out of. That's why there are fewer celebrities who come from talent shows than there are from reality shows. That's what you will have to fight against if you're going to become a celebrity that way.

And if you do, lots of us will be fascinated by you, because celebrity is fascinating. For we who watch, and for the celebrities themselves. Even the very famous, who've earned it through skill, through talent, through genuine hard work and rising up through the ranks of their chosen profession, are not immune to the fascination of celebrity. Not every famous person is content with being recognised for their talent. Many of them want the magic dust of celebrity as well.

Take the phenomenon of dark glasses. Have you ever genuinely not known who somebody was because they had sunglasses on? No, and neither have I. Adding a baseball cap doesn't make a person any less recognisable either. Think about it: would you pay more attention to a person walking by, with or without make-up, hair flowing free, walking with a normal stride and not looking anywhere but where they're going, or a person checking furtively around as they walk, eyes hidden by the blackest of lenses? The answer is that, of course, the second type of person will draw far more attention to themselves.

So, why do they do it, you might wonder — though not for long. It's obvious that they do it because they want to be recognised; they want us to look at them in the street for that little bit longer, they want to see the look of 'who's that?' on our faces, and even more than that, they love the look that comes next — that they hope will come next — the one that says, 'oh, it's that bloke off the telly'. Then they are happy and can continue to go about their day, searching the crowds, looking for the next person who will go through the same moment of puzzlement and recognition.

There's a story that may or may not be true — but probably is — about Kenneth Williams (ask your parents if you don't know who he is). The man was a British star, no question. He was known as an actor in the Carry On films, the nation echoed with his catch-phrases, 'Ooh, Matron' and 'Stop messing about', and that wasn't all he was known for. In the days when there were only two or three television channels, Williams was quickly recognised for his sharp wit and ability to tell a hilarious anecdote. He read a generation of children stories on *Jackanory*, meaning he was known to adults and kids alike. He was surely as famous as anyone could have been at that time, yet he was known to do a thing in restaurants that suggests no amount of fame was quite enough. He would sit quietly, eating or perusing the menu, and if nobody noticed him, he'd start being very loud, his distinctive nasal tone discussing the menu with his companion, or demanding more wine from the waiter, until finally people would recognise him and start nudging each other, pointing at him, and as soon as that started, he would leave. So it doesn't matter how famous you are, you might still need more. More of that attention from strangers, more adoration, or disdain, or whatever it is the public feels about you.

Williams wasn't alone in this behaviour — then, as now, it happens a lot. The cliché about the well-known person trying to get to the front of the queue, or a discount in Harrods, screeching, 'Don't you know who I am?', had to come from somewhere. Though nowadays, I would like to think celebrities could come up with a more original line. Still, there's no doubt that any kind of celebrity is useful for getting the best tables in restaurants, and seats to the sold-out shows in the West End.

Certain famous couples spring to mind, such

as Brangelina, who are fascinated with their own celebrity. How often do we see photos of such couples at an airport, dark glasses on, children around their feet? Are we meant to believe these people can't get quietly and quickly ushered through Heathrow with the minimum of fuss? Other famous people get on planes, and we don't see photos of them doing it splashed all over our breakfast read. We know the names of all of the children — and there are quite a few — of both couples; we know the dating histories of all four of them; we know what surgeries the women have both had. Well, we think we do. We know about enough of them.

Think about other actors and so-called stars — when did we ever see a shot of Kathy Bates waiting for a plane? Of Julia Roberts, Keira Knightley? Do we know the names of Matt Damon's children? Of Susan Sarandon's? Kevin Bacon's? Without looking them up on Wikipedia, I mean. The answer is no, because they haven't chosen to live their lives with the press paying for and documenting their every move. Of course you'll get the odd paparazzi shot of almost everybody, there are too many ways to find people these days, but mostly it's a choice. For a lot of actors and singers, being successful in their work — and the fame that might bring with it — is enough. For many more, it isn't. They are addicted to the adoration they believe they should be getting, and will do everything they can to get more of it. A psychologist could probably explain why, but I'm not going to begin to try.

The point is, celebrity is addictive. The celebrities we are talking about — the kind you can be — feel that addiction on a different level. They have done nothing to earn it, but they really, really want it, and in today's society, they feel that should be enough. They want the Hollywood glamour, they want the flashing lights, the red carpet, the after-party. Never mind that when it's over, they'll stagger back to their room at the Travelodge, then get up in the morning and go back to their humdrum life, sitting waiting for the phone to ring with details of the next premiere that the promoters are having trouble filling with celebs. *Kung Fu Panda 7*? Yes, please!

If this is what you want, then jump on board. There will be a demand for and a celebration of you. It might be negative, it's less likely to be positive, but if you get through all the points previously discussed, it will be there for you. But it will end. And that will be fine, won't it, because you've done all the things I've said. You've put aside your money, you've got your qualifications, and you have a whole other fulfilling life to fall back on. Haven't you?

8
The downside of fame

Hard to believe, I know, but it's not all posh restaurants and red carpets. For every dinner at The Ivy, there's a night alone watching other famous people on the telly, bitterly wondering why you're not there. But that's not the downside I'm talking about. I'm talking about something darker and altogether more sinister. Something depressing, sometimes even scary. I'm talking about the attention you don't want.

This comes in two main forms, the first of which is the stalker. Stalkers come in all shapes and sizes, and they can go for any kind of celebrity. There are extremes like John Hinckley Jr who famously shot Ronald Reagan, the then President of the United States, in order to get the attention of actress Jodie Foster. What you may not know is that this wasn't Hinckley's first attempt at making Foster notice him; he actually enrolled in a writing class at Yale while she was there, hoping that they would make a connection in class. He couldn't have done this if he wasn't highly intelligent, so don't make the mistake of thinking stalkers are stupid; they can be very bright, and therefore more dangerous. Most commonly, though, they think they are in love with the person they're stalking. There's a psychological name for this — it's called erotomania, and is characterised by the fact that the stalker believes they are actually in a relationship with the person they are stalking. Madonna famously had one of these, and the radio DJ Mike Read had one called Blue Tulip, who would turn up at recordings and in the lobby of Capital Radio when he worked there, saying, 'I've come to see my husband.' She seemed to truly believe she was married to him and, if she did manage to catch him, she would start discussing things about their life together, which didn't exist. It must have been quite scary.

Stalkers have always been around, but these days it's so much easier for them. A bit of knowledge about how to negotiate your way around the Internet means anybody can find out quite a lot about you. If you've sold half your life to the papers and gossip mags, it's even easier for them. In fact, it's not surprising people feel they know you, when they know everything about you. But if one of those people is a stalker, you could be in for some serious trouble. Stalkers are not fun, and they do exist.

Another unpleasant side of fame comes from much closer to home. Friends and family. Yes, you read that right — you think you know who your friends are, which family members you can trust, and if you never become a celebrity you will probably never have to question that. However, if you do manage to achieve your goal of celebrity status, you may be shocked at how those who profess to care about you can react. If you have a skeleton in your closet, a single bad thing in your history, you need to seriously consider telling the press about it, because if you don't, you can bet your boots someone in your life will.

If you've done drugs, if you've been naughty, if you've slept around, if people don't like you, if you've got a police record, if you just have something in your life you wouldn't want people to know about, the chances are the press will find out. Somebody, once you become famous, will sell you down the river. If they go to a paper and say, 'I know something about her', the journalist will ask if it's any good, and then they tell them — just wondering if they'd be interested; just seeing how much it would be worth if they did talk — and the journalist says, 'That's worth ten grand'. How good a friend would they have to be to decide their relationship with you is worth more than that? What if they're just somebody you've met a couple of times and overshared with? They'll take that money and your time will be up. It's an old, tried and tested way of making news and it's so easy to do with the kind of celebrity you will be. They've been doing it to the famous since the dawn of newspapers.

Back in the 1970s, there was a popular and very successful talk-show host called Russell Harty, who happened to be gay in a time when famous people would never admit to being gay. Apart from it ending his career, he didn't want his mother to know. In 1987, the now defunct

News of the World found out he was seeing a rent boy, because the rent boy told them, and agreed to be miked up for their next rendezvous. Of course it didn't occur to Harty that the boy would be recording his every word, and he spilled his heart out to him, and that was that. The paper shouted it from its front pages and the man's career was over. He was mortified, and only relieved that his mother was dead by the time it happened. Although people loved him, the scandal destroyed him. You won't be so loved, you won't be so protected, you will hopefully know better than to trust someone who has been paid to spend time with you, but you will not be immune from having your secrets splashed all over the gossip mags and rags.

There are people who plant stories about themselves, just to keep the flame of celebrity burning, but she's canny. They know what scandals they want us to know about and what secrets they want to keep to themselves. They've been at this a long time, and have learned from being burned. You won't have that longevity because, as we've established, you are planning on being famous for being famous (Jordan did this first, which makes her different. Also, she cashed in on her time as a Page Three girl). You won't be around long enough to pick and choose what the press gets to know. And if you've got anyone in your past who doesn't have a watertight commitment to you, you will be the subject of negative stories. But you won't mind that, will you, because it comes with the territory. You know it's inevitable, and it's just part of this new kind of fame. This celebrity. They do it to the Kardashians, so surely it's just fine that they do it to you, too.

The kind of fame you will have will not be about people universally loving you. Some will (unless you do the Josie Cunningham thing), and a lot of young teenagers may well want to be you. Some people older than that might find you charming, amusing, kind-hearted even, but a lot of people will have a kind of morbid fascination. A wonder at how you managed to get there, a curiosity about how long it will last, and a kind of resignation to the fact that you're just another one of these modern celebrity people who have done nothing to get where you appear to be.

I'm one of those people, as anybody who listens to my show will know. I have a morbid fascination and incredulous disbelief that this is still going on. My boss always says to me, 'Do you really hate all these people?' and I say no. Because I don't hate them; they form the basis of most of what I watch on the television, I'm as sucked in as anybody else. And like everybody else, I'm watching and saying to myself, 'Oh God, it's that bloody person again.'

I was watching a series of *Big Brother*, for instance, and there were some awful people in there, including a prostitute who slept with Wayne Rooney, and she was just vile, but they kept her in for exactly that reason. I understand how the system works, but at the same time I can't help but think they were just fuelling her fantasy of being famous, making her believe that she was, and the crowd booed, and everyone hated her, but the papers wrote about her, and that's what the programme makers wanted. It's what she wanted. And we all kept watching, and another celebrity was born before our eyes.

9

So why do I want to do this again?

Why do you want to do any of this? I don't know, really. I do know it doesn't interest me, but then I'm not really the benchmark. I'm just saying that, for me, it holds no interest. I couldn't think of anything worse, especially now I've written it all down, but then I consider myself lucky. I'm happy that I've had a career I love, that has lasted so long, but I'm not well known — I'm well known to people in my field, people who do what I do, or are associated with it, and that's as far as I want to go. If I'm recognised a couple of times a week, that's more than enough for me. If somebody wants to talk to me or somebody writes in saying they like the programme, that's lovely. If somebody says 'What you do is good', I think, 'That's fine. I earn some money, I have my own home, thank you very much indeed.' That is me satisfied. I have a great life, and I'm happy.

I don't know why people crave celebrity, I really don't. I don't believe the line that 'all children today want to be famous', because I've met plenty of children who don't want that at all, but I do believe that more people than ever before do want it. More people in their late teens and early twenties want to be famous today, and there are these routes that they can take. Perhaps they have something missing in their life, perhaps they see these modern-day celebrities and think they're glamorous and fabulous. Well, I can tell you that when you meet them, they have very little of interest to talk about. The thing is, they got their dream, they're just ordinary people who had a camera thrust in their face and loved it, they learned how to pose and how to look like they're having a better time than the rest of us, and it worked. People do that, and they will probably do it for a long time to come. I see no end in sight at the moment. As television becomes cheaper and cheaper — and reality shows are the cheapest programmes to make — and people still want so desperately to have their shot at being famous, it won't end. If you put out a press release saying 'We need twelve people to appear stark naked with their mothers on their heads by 1 p.m. this afternoon', you'd have a queue around the block.

People who want it will do anything — they will queue to be famous, they crave that thing. And I can't pretend to understand it, I can only come up with my own theories from what I've observed.

Having come to the end of this book, I can say one thing with certainty. No matter what you might think of celebrities, having read through these pages, it is beyond doubt that they will keep on dominating our media, and our attention, for the foreseeable future. We can't stop looking — whether we find them good or bad, or we're indifferent; whether they're going wild on drugs or alcohol or we can't tear ourselves away from their domestic dramas — celebrities still make up some 80 per cent of our daily magazine and newspaper coverage.

And they will continue to do so for many years to come.

About LBC

LBC is Britain's only national news talk radio station. It tackles the big issues of the day, with intelligent, informed and provocative opinion from guests, listeners and presenters, including Nick Ferrari, James O'Brien, Shelagh Fogarty, Iain Dale, Ken Livingstone, David Mellor and Beverley Turner. LBC reaches 1.2 million people in Britain and is available on DAB digital radio, online at lbc.co.uk, through mobile apps, Sky Digital Channel 0112, Virgin Media Channel 919 and on 97.3FM in London.

About the Series

In this major new series, popular LBC presenters tackle the big issues in politics, current affairs and society. We might applaud their views; we might be outraged. But these short, sharp polemics are destined to generate controversy, discussion and debate — and lead Britain's conversation.

Titles in the series

Steve Allen, *So You Want to Be a Celebrity?*
Duncan Barkes, *The Dumbing Down of Britain*
Iain Dale, *The NHS: Things That Need to Be Said*
Nick Ferrari, *It's Politics ... But Not As We Know It*
James O'Brien, *Loathe Thy Neighbour*